DIASPORA PROPERTY FORMULA™

IMPLEMENTATION WORKBOOK

Your Trusted System for Safe Property Investment in Nigeria — From Anywhere in the World

A Companion Guide to the *#1* International Bestseller

Abiodun D. Doherty

Copyright © 2025 by Abiodun D. Doherty. All rights reserved.

No part of this publication may be reproduced, distributed, or transmitted in any form or by any means, including photocopying, recording, or other electronic or mechanical methods, without the prior written permission of the publisher, except in the case of brief quotations embodied in critical reviews and certain other noncommercial uses permitted by copyright law.

Disclaimer: This workbook is a companion guide to the book, *Diaspora Property Formula*. It provides tools, worksheets, and prompts for educational and informational purposes only. It is not intended as a substitute for professional legal, financial, or real estate advice. Always consult with a qualified legal practitioner or licensed financial advisor before making investment decisions.

Published by: Abiodun Doherty
First Edition: 2025

ISBN (Paperback): 978-1-7643149-2-3

Website: www.diasporapropertyformula.com
Support Email: info@diasporapropertyformula.com

WELCOME TO THE IMPLEMENTATION PHASE

Turning Knowledge into Net Worth

The Diaspora Property Formula™ is more than just a book—it is a proven system designed to replace fear and speculation with confidence and profit. Congratulations on taking the next essential step: Implementation.

The knowledge in the book has shown you *what* to do. This workbook is the essential tool that shows you how to do it. It is your personal action planner, guiding you from theoretical understanding to verified, signed, and profitable property ownership in Nigeria.

This workbook is structured to mirror the journey of the book, giving you specific action steps, checklists, and planning sheets for every major theme. Whether you are identifying your first investment or scaling your existing portfolio, use these pages to document your strategy and verify every critical decision.

Your success depends on implementation.

Let's get to work.

YOUR BLUEPRINT FOR ACTION

Instructions on Maximizing Results

This workbook is designed for **active use**. Follow these steps to maximize your results:

- **Read the Core Chapter First:** Before starting a section in this workbook, ensure you have read the corresponding chapter in *The Diaspora Property Formula*. This provides the context and principles necessary for the exercises.

- **Choose Your Format:** This workbook is designed to be fully writable. Print it out and use a pen, or use a PDF editor to fill in the spaces digitally.

- **Prioritize Verification:** The prompts, checklists, and worksheets are not optional—they are your **proof of due diligence**. Do not proceed to the next chapter's tools until you have completed the action items in the current one.

- **Date Everything:** Always date your assessments and action plans (e.g., *Date of Assessment: 11/10/2025*). This is crucial for tracking remote investment progress.

- **Review Regularly:** Set aside time monthly to review your progress and adjust your strategy.

Insight from the DPF:

"Peace of mind is not a luxury in property investment; it is the foundation of profitable investment."

— Abiodun D. Doherty

TABLE OF CONTENTS

WELCOME TO THE IMPLEMENTATION PHASE III

YOUR BLUEPRINT FOR ACTION IV

CHAPTER 1: SELF-ASSESSMENT 1

CHAPTER 2: THE PROPERTY TRAPS YOU MUST AVOID 7

CHAPTER 3: PICKING THE RIGHT LOCATION 15

CHAPTER 4: LEGAL LANDMINES AND HOW TO AVOID THEM 21

CHAPTER 5: FINANCING STRATEGY PLANNER 26

CHAPTER 6: DPF HOTSPOT RADAR TOOL 33

CHAPTER 7: TEAM BUILDING TEMPLATE 42

CHAPTER 8: REMOTE MANAGEMENT CHECKLIST 53

CHAPTER 9: YOUR 90-DAY IMPLEMENTATION JOURNEY 63

CHAPTER 10: PROGRESS TRACKING & WINS TRACKER 83

ABOUT THE AUTHOR 87

JOIN THE ACADEMY 88

NOTES & REFLECTIONS 91

CHAPTER 1

SELF-ASSESSMENT

Are You Ready to Invest?

FROM THE BOOK:

Before you invest a single naira in Nigerian property, you must conduct an honest self-assessment. Many diaspora Nigerians rush into property investment driven by emotion, family pressure, or FOMO (fear of missing out), only to face devastating losses. The Diaspora Property Formula emphasizes that successful investment begins with readiness—financial, knowledge-based, and psychological.

This chapter walks you through a comprehensive self-evaluation across five critical dimensions: your financial foundation, knowledge acquisition, professional network, analytical capabilities, and implementation readiness. Only when you score adequately across all dimensions should you proceed with confidence. Remember: it's better to wait 12 months and invest wisely than to rush in unprepared and lose your hard-earned capital.

SELF-ASSESSMENT TRACKER

Current Date: _____

Assessment Period: _____

Next Review Date: _____

FINANCIAL FOUNDATION

Rate yourself from 1 (Not Ready) to 5 (Fully Ready):

Financial Element	Score (1-5)	Target	Gap	Action Needed
Emergency fund (6 months expenses)	_____	5	___	
Debt-to-income ratio (<30%)	_____	5	___	
Investment capital availability	_____	4	___	
Multiple income streams	_____	3	___	
Financial literacy level	_____	4	___	
Foundation Subtotal	_____/25	21		

Notes on Financial Foundation:

_____

_____

_____

PHASE 2: KNOWLEDGE ACQUISITION

Rate your understanding from 1 (No Knowledge) to 5 (Expert Level):

Knowledge Area	Score (1-5)	Target	Gap	Learning Plan
Nigerian property market	_____	4	___	
Legal requirements	_____	4	___	
Investment locations	_____	3	___	
Property management	_____	3	___	
Exit strategies	_____	3	___	

Knowledge Area	Score (1-5)	Target	Gap	Learning Plan
Tax implications	_____	4	___	
Knowledge Subtotal	_____/30	21		

Books/Resources to Complete:

_____

_____

_____

PHASE 3: NETWORK DEVELOPMENT

Rate your network strength from 1 (No Contacts) to 5 (Strong Network):

Network Element	Score (1-5)	Target	Gap	Development Plan
Real estate agents	_____	4	___	
Legal counsel	_____	4	___	
Property managers	_____	3	___	
Local connections	_____	3	___	
Diaspora community	_____	3	___	
Financial advisors	_____	3	___	
Network Subtotal	_____/30	20		

Networking Actions This Month:

_____

_____

_____

PHASE 4: MARKET ANALYSIS CAPABILITY

Rate your capability from 1 (Cannot Analyze) to 5 (Expert Analysis):

Analysis Capability	Score (1-5)	Target	Gap	Development Need
Location evaluation	_____	4	___	
Property valuation	_____	3	___	
Rental yield calculation	_____	3	___	
Risk assessment	_____	4	___	
Market trend analysis	_____	3	___	
Due diligence process	_____	4	___	
Analysis Subtotal	_____/30	21		

Skills to Develop This Quarter:

_____

_____

_____

PHASE 5: IMPLEMENTATION READINESS

Rate your readiness from 1 (Not Ready) to 5 (Fully Ready):

Implementation Element	Score (1-5)	Target	Gap	Preparation Needed
Decision-making confidence	_____	4	___	
Execution timeline clarity	_____	3	___	
Resource allocation plan	_____	4	___	

Implementation Element	Score (1-5)	Target	Gap	Preparation Needed
Risk tolerance defined	_____	3	___	
Commitment level	_____	5	___	
Implementation Subtotal	_____/25	19		

DPF READINESS SCORE

TOTAL SCORE: _____ /140

TARGET SCORE: 102/140 (73%)

READINESS ASSESSMENT

Your Investment Readiness Level:

- **112-140 points**

  READY TO INVEST
  You have the financial foundation, knowledge, and systems to proceed. Begin searching for opportunities actively.

- **84-111 points**

  NEARLY READY
  You're close but need to address weak areas. Focus on gaps identified above. Timeline to readiness: 2-3 months.

- **56-83 points**

  SIGNIFICANT PREPARATION NEEDED
  Major groundwork required before investing. Rushing now could be costly. Timeline: 4-6 months.

- **Below 56 points**

  NOT READY
  Premature investment poses high risk. Focus intensively on Phases 1-2. Timeline: 6-12 months.

PRIORITY IMPROVEMENT AREAS

Top 3 Areas Requiring Focus:

1. _____ (Current Score: ____/5, Target: ____/5)

    Action Plan: _____

2. _____ (Current Score: ____/5, Target: ____/5)

    Action Plan: _____

3. _____ (Current Score: ____/5, Target: ____/5)

    Action Plan: _____

ACCOUNTABILITY COMMITMENT

I commit to reviewing this assessment on:

- **Monthly:** _____ (date)
- **Quarterly:** _____ (date)
- **Annually:** _____ (date)

Accountability Partner: _____

Contact: _____

Signature: _____ Date: _____

CHAPTER 2

THE PROPERTY TRAPS YOU MUST AVOID

FROM THE BOOK:

Nigerian property investment is fraught with traps that have cost diaspora investors billions of naira. From fraudulent developers and fake title documents to inflated prices and hidden legal issues, the landscape is treacherous for the uninformed. This chapter reveals the most common and costly mistakes diaspora investors make—and more importantly, how to avoid them.

The DPF system emphasizes systematic risk assessment before every investment decision. You'll learn to evaluate financial risks (pricing, hidden costs, currency fluctuations), legal risks (title clarity, government approvals, dispute history), and location risks (infrastructure, security, market saturation). By completing the Risk Assessment Worksheet for every property, you create documented proof of due diligence and dramatically reduce your chances of catastrophic loss. Remember: the goal isn't to eliminate all risk—that's impossible—but to identify, quantify, and manage risk within acceptable parameters.

RISK ASSESSMENT WORKSHEET

Property Details:

- **Property Address:** _____

- **Property Type:** ☐ Land ☐ House ☐ Apartment ☐ Commercial

- **Purchase Price:** ₦ _____ ($ _____)

- **Developer/Seller:** _____

- **Date of Assessment:** _____

FINANCIAL RISK ASSESSMENT

Rate each factor from 1 (Low Risk) to 5 (High Risk):

Risk Factor	Score (1-5)	Notes/Evidence
Purchase price vs market value	_____	
Hidden costs and fees	_____	
Currency exchange fluctuation	_____	
Rental yield projections	_____	
Exit strategy viability	_____	
Financial Risk Subtotal	_____/25	

Key Financial Concerns:

_____

_____

_____

LEGAL RISK ASSESSMENT

Rate each factor from 1 (Low Risk) to 5 (High Risk):

Risk Factor	Score (1-5)	Notes/Evidence
Title documentation clarity	_____	
Government approval status	_____	
Land dispute history	_____	
Developer track record	_____	
Legal compliance verification	_____	
Legal Risk Subtotal	_____/25	

Key Legal Concerns:

_____

_____

_____

LOCATION RISK ASSESSMENT

Rate each factor from 1 (Low Risk) to 5 (High Risk):

Risk Factor	Score (1-5)	Notes/Evidence
Area development plans	_____	
Infrastructure reliability	_____	
Security concerns	_____	
Market saturation	_____	
Accessibility and transportation	_____	
Location Risk Subtotal	_____/25	

Key Location Concerns:

_____

_____

_____

TOTAL RISK SCORE: _____ /75

RISK LEVEL INTERPRETATION:

- **15-30 points:**

    LOW RISK - Proceed with confidence

- **31-45 points:**

    MODERATE RISK - Address concerns before proceeding

- **46-60 points:**

    HIGH RISK - Significant risk mitigation required

- **61-75 points:**

    VERY HIGH RISK - Strongly consider walking away

DECISION MATRIX

Based on your total risk score, what action will you take?

- **PROCEED** - Move forward with investment
- **CONDITIONAL** - Proceed only after addressing these specific issues:

1. _____

2. _____

3. _____

- **NEGOTIATE** - Renegotiate terms to reduce risk in these areas:

4. _____

5. _____

- **WALK AWAY** - Risk too high; find better opportunity

Deadline for Final Decision: _____

Decision Maker(s): _____

PROFESSIONAL TEAM CHECKLIST

REAL ESTATE AGENT/CONSULTANT

- Licensed and registered with appropriate bodies
- Minimum 3 years experience in target area
- Proven track record with diaspora clients
- References from at least 3 previous clients
- Clear fee structure and written agreement
- Responsive communication (responds within 24 hours)

Agent Details:

- Name: _____
- License Number: _____
- Years of Experience: _____
- Contact Information: _____

LEGAL COUNSEL/LAWYER

- Nigerian Bar Association member in good standing
- Specializes in property/real estate law
- Experience with foreign investor transactions
- Clear fee structure for all services
- Available for ongoing consultation

Lawyer Details:

- Name: _____
- Bar Number: _____
- Law Firm: _____
- Contact Information: _____

PROPERTY MANAGER

- Licensed property management company
- Comprehensive service offerings
- Technology-enabled reporting systems
- Emergency response procedures
- Transparent fee structure
- Regular inspection and maintenance protocols

Property Manager Details:

- Company Name: _____
- License Number: _____
- Services Included: _____
- Monthly Fee: _____

FINANCIAL ADVISOR/ACCOUNTANT

- Professional accounting body membership
- Tax expertise for international clients
- Understanding of Nigerian property taxation
- Experience with foreign exchange management
- Investment planning capabilities

Accountant Details:

- Name: _____
- Professional Body: _____
- Specialization: _____
- Contact Information: _____

DUE DILIGENCE TEMPLATES

DOCUMENT VERIFICATION CHECKLIST

Essential Documents:

- Certificate of Occupancy (C of O)
- Survey Plan
- Building Plan Approval
- Environmental Impact Assessment (if applicable)
- Tax clearance certificates
- Power of Attorney (if applicable)
- Purchase Receipt/Agreement
- Development Control Approval

Document Status:

- Original Available: ☐ Yes ☐ No
- Certified True Copies: ☐ Yes ☐ No
- Legal Verification Complete: ☐ Yes ☐ No

Verified By: _____ **Date:** _____

PROPERTY INSPECTION CHECKLIST

Structural Assessment:

- Foundation condition - Rating: _____/10
- Wall integrity and finishing - Rating: _____/10
- Roofing condition - Rating: _____/10
- Electrical installations - Rating: _____/10
- Plumbing systems - Rating: _____/10
- Windows and doors - Rating: _____/10
- Flooring condition - Rating: _____/10

Infrastructure Assessment:

- Access roads condition - Rating: _____/10
- Electricity supply reliability - Rating: _____/10
- Water supply availability - Rating: _____/10
- Drainage systems - Rating: _____/10
- Security infrastructure - Rating: _____/10
- Telecommunications access - Rating: _____/10

Neighborhood Assessment:

- Development level of area - Rating: _____/10
- Proximity to amenities - Rating: _____/10
- Transportation links - Rating: _____/10
- Safety and security - Rating: _____/10
- Future development plans - Rating: _____/10
- Property value trends - Rating: _____/10

Overall Property Rating: _____/10

Inspector: _____ **Date:** _____

CHAPTER 3

PICKING THE RIGHT LOCATION

FROM THE BOOK:

In Nigerian real estate, location isn't just important—it's everything. The difference between a property that doubles in value and one that stagnates for a decade often comes down to location selection. Yet many diaspora investors choose locations based on nostalgia, family pressure, or incomplete information rather than systematic analysis.

The DPF 5-Point Location Scorecard evaluates every potential investment area across five weighted dimensions: infrastructure development, economic growth potential, accessibility, amenities, and security. Each factor is scored and weighted according to its impact on property value and rental income. A location scoring 390+ points represents an excellent investment opportunity, while anything below 196 should raise serious concerns. This systematic approach removes emotion from the equation and ensures your capital flows to areas with the highest probability of strong returns. Location analysis isn't glamorous, but it's the foundation of every successful property investment.

5-POINT LOCATION SCORECARD

Location Being Assessed: _____

Date of Assessment: _____

Assessed By: _____

1. INFRASTRUCTURE DEVELOPMENT

Rate from 1 (Poor) to 10 (Excellent):

Infrastructure Element	Score (1-10)	Weight	Weighted Score
Road networks	_____	x2 =	_____ /20
Electricity supply	_____	x3 =	_____ /30
Water supply	_____	x2 =	_____ /20
Internet/telecommunications	_____	x1 =	_____ /10
Drainage systems	_____	x1 =	_____ /10
Infrastructure Subtotal			**_____ /90**

Notes on Infrastructure:

_____

_____

_____

2. ECONOMIC GROWTH POTENTIAL

Rate from 1 (Poor) to 10 (Excellent):

Economic Factor	Score (1-10)	Weight	Weighted Score
Job creation opportunities	_____	x3 =	_____ /30
Business district proximity	_____	x2 =	_____ /20
Government investment plans	_____	x2 =	_____ /20
Population growth trends	_____	x2 =	_____ /20
Income level of residents	_____	x1 =	_____ /10
Economic Subtotal			_____/100

Notes on Economic Potential:

_____

_____

_____

3. ACCESSIBILITY & TRANSPORTATION

Rate from 1 (Poor) to 10 (Excellent):

Transportation Factor	Score (1-10)	Weight	Weighted Score
Airport proximity	_____	x2 =	_____ /20
Major highway access	_____	x3 =	_____ /30
Public transportation	_____	x2 =	_____ /20
Traffic congestion (reverse score)	_____	x2 =	_____ /20
Parking availability	_____	x1 =	_____ /10
Accessibility Subtotal			_____/100

Notes on Accessibility:

_____

_____

_____

4. AMENITIES & LIFESTYLE

Rate from 1 (Poor) to 10 (Excellent):

Amenity Factor	Score (1-10)	Weight	Weighted Score
Schools quality	_____	x3 =	_____ /30
Healthcare facilities	_____	x2 =	_____ /20
Shopping centers	_____	x2 =	_____ /20
Recreation facilities	_____	x1 =	_____ /10
Religious centers	_____	x1 =	_____ /10
Banks/financial services	_____	x1 =	_____ /10
Amenities Subtotal			_____/100

Notes on Amenities:

_____

_____

_____

5. SECURITY & SAFETY

Rate from 1 (Poor) to 10 (Excellent):

Security Factor	Score (1-10)	Weight	Weighted Score
Crime rates (reverse score)	_____	x3 =	_____ /30
Police presence	_____	x2 =	_____ /20
Street lighting	_____	x2 =	_____ /20
Gated community features	_____	x2 =	_____ /20
Emergency services access	_____	x1 =	_____ /10
Security Subtotal			**_____/100**

Notes on Security:

_____

_____

_____

LOCATION SCORECARD SUMMARY

Category	Your Score	Maximum	Percentage
Infrastructure	_____	90	_____%
Economic Growth	_____	100	_____%
Accessibility	_____	100	_____%
Amenities	_____	100	_____%
Security	_____	100	_____%
TOTAL SCORE	_____	**490**	_____%

LOCATION RATING

Your Score: _____ /490

- **390-490 points:** ☆☆☆☆☆ **Excellent location** - Strong investment potential
- **294-389 points:** ☆☆☆☆ **Good location** - Recommended with confidence
- **196-293 points:** ☆☆☆ **Average location** - Acceptable with proper due diligence
- **98-195 points:** ☆☆ **Below average** - Requires compelling reason to proceed
- **Below 98 points:** ☆ **Poor location** - Not recommended

INVESTMENT RECOMMENDATION

- **Strongly Recommend** - Excellent opportunity
- **Recommend with Conditions** - Good but address:

- **Consider Alternatives** - Better options likely available
- **Do Not Recommend** - Risk outweighs potential reward

Final Assessment:

_____

_____

_____

Assessor: _____ Date: _____

CHAPTER 4

LEGAL LANDMINES AND HOW TO AVOID THEM

FROM THE BOOK:

The legal landscape of Nigerian property ownership is complex, bureaucratic, and fraught with potential catastrophes for the uninformed. From fake Certificates of Occupancy to family land disputes, from "omo onile" extortion to missing Governor's Consent, the legal pitfalls are numerous and expensive. This is why the majority of diaspora property losses occur not from bad locations or poor timing, but from inadequate legal protection.

The DPF Legal Checklist is your non-negotiable safeguard against legal disaster. It systematically verifies every critical legal requirement: title documentation authenticity, government approvals, developer credibility, purchase agreement terms, regulatory compliance, and post-purchase registration obligations. Every checkbox represents a potential six-figure loss if ignored. Your lawyer should complete this checklist for every property under consideration—and if they resist or rush through it, find a new lawyer. Legal due diligence isn't an expense; it's insurance against catastrophic loss. In Nigerian property investment, cutting legal corners doesn't save money—it guarantees you'll lose it.

COMPREHENSIVE LEGAL CHECKLIST

Property Information:

- Property Address: _____
- Property Type: _____
- Developer/Seller: _____
- Transaction Date: _____
- Legal Counsel: _____

PRE-PURCHASE LEGAL VERIFICATION

TITLE DOCUMENTATION:

- Certificate of Occupancy verified as authentic
- Survey plan matches property boundaries exactly
- Chain of title is clear and unbroken
- No encumbrances or liens on property
- Title search conducted at Land Registry
- No pending litigation on property
- All previous owners identified and verified

Verification Date: _____ **Verified By:** _____

GOVERNMENT APPROVALS:

- Building plan approval obtained and current
- Development permit verified with authorities
- Environmental clearance (if required by law)
- Change of use approval (if applicable)
- All applicable taxes and levies paid and current
- Local government consent obtained
- State government approvals in place

Verification Date: _____ **Verified By:** _____

DEVELOPER/SELLER VERIFICATION:

- Company registration verified with CAC
- Developer track record investigated thoroughly
- Financial capacity assessment completed
- Previous project delivery record checked
- Professional references obtained and verified
- Insurance and bonding status confirmed
- No history of fraud or litigation

Verification Date: _____ **Verified By:** _____

LEGAL DOCUMENTATION REVIEW

PURCHASE AGREEMENT ANALYSIS:

- All terms clearly defined in writing
- Payment schedule specified with dates
- Completion timeline established
- Penalty clauses for delays included
- Force majeure provisions reviewed
- Dispute resolution mechanism specified
- Termination conditions clearly stated
- Warranties and representations included

Reviewed By: _____ **Date:** _____

POWER OF ATTORNEY (if applicable):

- Properly executed and stamped
- Grantor verification completed
- Scope of authority clearly defined
- Registration requirements met
- Revocation provisions understood
- Expiration date noted

Reviewed By: _____ **Date:** _____

REGULATORY COMPLIANCE

ZONING AND LAND USE:

- Property zoning verified for intended use
- Building regulations compliance checked
- Setback requirements met
- Height restrictions observed
- Density regulations adhered to
- Environmental regulations complied with

Verified By: _____ **Date:** _____

TAX OBLIGATIONS:

- Property tax status verified and current
- Ground rent obligations understood
- Capital gains tax implications reviewed
- Stamp duty requirements understood and budgeted
- Annual returns filing obligations clear

Verified By: _____ **Date:** _____

POST-PURCHASE LEGAL ACTIONS

REGISTRATION REQUIREMENTS:

- Deed of assignment preparation scheduled
- Governor's consent application submitted
- Property registration at Land Registry initiated
- Tax identification number obtained
- Property insurance arranged
- Title documents secured safely

Completion Deadline: _____

OVERALL LEGAL RISK ASSESSMENT

- **LOW RISK**: Proceed with confidence

  All legal requirements satisfied. Documentation authentic and complete.

- **MODERATE RISK**: Address identified issues:

  1. _____

- 2. _____

- 3. _____

- **HIGH RISK**: Seek additional legal counsel

  Significant legal concerns require expert resolution.

- **UNACCEPTABLE RISK**: Do not proceed

  Legal issues make investment inadvisable.

Legal Advisor Confirmation:

"I have reviewed all documentation and completed the legal due diligence checklist. My professional opinion is documented above."

Lawyer Name: _____

Bar Number: _____

Date of Review: _____

Signature: _____

CHAPTER 5

FINANCING STRATEGY PLANNER

FROM THE BOOK:

How you finance your Nigerian property investment is as important as which property you buy. The wrong financing strategy can turn a good investment into a financial burden, while the right approach maximizes returns and manages risk effectively. Diaspora investors face unique financing challenges: currency exchange volatility, limited access to Nigerian mortgages, payment plan complexity, and the temptation to overextend financially.

This chapter guides you through a systematic financing analysis comparing four primary approaches: full cash payment, developer payment plans, Nigerian bank financing, and hybrid strategies. Each option has distinct advantages and risks that must be weighed against your specific financial situation, risk tolerance, and investment timeline. The Financing Strategy Planner helps you calculate the true cost of each option—including often-overlooked factors like currency hedging, opportunity cost, and financing fees—to determine your optimal approach. Remember: the cheapest financing isn't always the best, and cash isn't always king. Your goal is sustainable financing that supports long-term wealth building without creating unsustainable financial stress.

FINANCING STRATEGY PLANNER

Investment Details:

- Property Value: ₦ _____ ($ _____)

- Target Purchase Date: _____

- Available Capital: $ _____ / ₦ _____

- Monthly Investment Capacity: $ _____ / ₦ _____

- Current Exchange Rate: ₦ _____ / $1

OPTION 1: FULL CASH PAYMENT

Financial Details:

- Total Amount Required: ₦ _____

- Exchange Rate Impact: _____% potential variance

- Timeline to Accumulate: _____ months

- Opportunity Cost: ₦ _____

ADVANTAGES:

- No interest payments
- Faster transaction completion
- Stronger negotiating position
- No debt obligations
- Immediate ownership

DISADVANTAGES:

- Large capital requirement
- Currency exchange risk concentration
- Reduced investment diversification
- Opportunity cost on other investments
- Tied up capital for extended period

Total Cost: ₦ _____

OPTION 2: DEVELOPER PAYMENT PLAN

Payment Structure:

- Initial Deposit: ₦ _____ (_____%)

- Monthly Payment: ₦ _____

- Payment Period: _____ months

- Final Payment: ₦ _____

- Interest Rate: _____% per annum

- Total Interest Cost: ₦ _____

Payment Schedule:

Month	Payment Amount	Balance	Notes
0	₦_____	₦_____	Initial deposit
1-6	₦_____	₦_____	
7-12	₦_____	₦_____	
13-18	₦_____	₦_____	
19-24	₦_____	₦_____	

Month	Payment Amount	Balance	Notes
Final	₦_____	₦0	Completion

Total Cost: ₦ _____

OPTION 3: NIGERIAN BANK FINANCING

Loan Details:

- Loan Amount: ₦ _____
- Interest Rate: _____% per annum
- Loan Term: _____ years
- Monthly Payment: ₦ _____
- Required Down Payment: ₦ _____ (_____%)
- Processing Fees: ₦ _____
- Insurance Requirements: ₦ _____
- Total Interest Over Term: ₦ _____

Requirements:

- Nigerian bank account
- Proof of income
- Property valuation
- Legal documentation
- Life insurance
- Property insurance

Total Cost: ₦ _____

OPTION 4: HYBRID APPROACH

Funding Mix:

- Own Capital: ₦ _____ (_____%)

- Developer Financing: ₦ _____ (_____%)

- Bank Loan: ₦ _____ (_____%)

- Other Sources: ₦ _____ (_____%)

Total Investment: ₦ _____

Combined Interest Cost: ₦ _____

CURRENCY RISK MANAGEMENT

Hedge Strategy Selected:

- Forward exchange contracts
- Currency hedging instruments
- Staggered payment timing
- Local currency earning assets
- Mixed currency approach

Transfer Strategy:

- Provider: _____

- Fee per Transfer: $ _____

- Exchange Rate Margin: _____%

- Transfer Frequency: _____

- Total Transfer Costs: $ _____

COMPARATIVE ANALYSIS

Factor	Cash	Payment Plan	Bank Loan	Hybrid
Total Cost	₦_____	₦_____	₦_____	₦_____
Upfront Capital	₦_____	₦_____	₦_____	₦_____
Monthly Payment	₦0	₦_____	₦_____	₦_____
Timeline	___mo	___mo	___mo	___mo
Flexibility	__/5	__/5	__/5	__/5
Risk Level	__/5	__/5	__/5	__/5

RECOMMENDED FINANCING STRATEGY

Selected Approach:

- Full Cash Payment
- Developer Payment Plan
- Nigerian Bank Financing
- Hybrid Approach
- Other: _____

Justification:

_____

_____

_____

_____

_____

IMPLEMENTATION TIMELINE

Month 1: _____

Month 2: _____

Month 3: _____

Month 4: _____

Month 5: _____

Month 6: _____

Completion Target: _____

TOTAL INVESTMENT COST SUMMARY

Cost Category	Amount (₦)	Amount ($)	Notes
Property Price			
Financing Costs			
Legal Fees			
Survey Fees			
Registration Fees			
Agent Commission			
Stamp Duty			
Insurance (Annual)			
Transfer Fees			
Contingency (10%)			
TOTAL INVESTMENT	₦_____	$_____	

Prepared By: _____ Date: _____

CHAPTER 6

DPF HOTSPOT RADAR TOOL

FROM THE BOOK:

Not all Nigerian cities and neighborhoods are created equal when it comes to property investment returns. While Lagos and Abuja dominate headlines and attract the majority of diaspora capital, savvy investors know that exceptional returns often lie in carefully selected secondary and emerging markets. The key is systematic market intelligence—knowing where infrastructure development, economic growth, and demographic trends are converging to create investment opportunities.

The DPF Hotspot Radar Tool helps you track and compare investment opportunities across Nigeria's primary markets (Lagos, Abuja), secondary markets (Port Harcourt, Kano, Ibadan), and emerging locations where early investment can yield outsized returns. For each market, you'll assess rental yields, capital appreciation trends, entry costs, infrastructure development, and risk levels. This tool transforms market research from overwhelming complexity into actionable intelligence. Update it quarterly to stay current with market dynamics, and use it to build a diversified portfolio across multiple locations and risk profiles. Remember: geographic diversification within Nigeria is as important as international diversification—it protects you from location-specific risks while maximizing your exposure to growth opportunities.

DPF HOTSPOT RADAR TOOL

Market Research Date: _____

Researcher: _____

Next Update Due: _____

PRIMARY MARKETS ANALYSIS

LAGOS STATE

Victoria Island/Ikoyi

- Current Rental Yield: _____% annually
- 3-Year Capital Appreciation: _____%
- Entry Cost Range: ₦ _____ to ₦ _____
- Market Maturity: ☐ Emerging ☐ Growing ☐ Mature ☐ Saturated
- Infrastructure Rating: _____/10
- ROI Potential: ☐ High ☐ Medium ☐ Low

Investment Verdict: ☐ Buy ☐ Hold ☐ Avoid

Notes: _____

_____

_____

Lekki Peninsula

- Current Rental Yield: _____% annually
- 3-Year Capital Appreciation: _____%
- Entry Cost Range: ₦ _____ to ₦ _____
- Market Maturity: ☐ Emerging ☐ Growing ☐ Mature ☐ Saturated
- Infrastructure Rating: _____/10
- ROI Potential: ☐ High ☐ Medium ☐ Low

Investment Verdict: ☐ Buy ☐ Hold ☐ Avoid

Notes: _____

_____

_____

Mainland Lagos (Ikeja/Maryland/Gbagada)

- Current Rental Yield: _____% annually
- 3-Year Capital Appreciation: _____%
- Entry Cost Range: ₦ _____ to ₦ _____
- Market Maturity: ☐ Emerging ☐ Growing ☐ Mature ☐ Saturated
- Infrastructure Rating: _____/10
- ROI Potential: ☐ High ☐ Medium ☐ Low

Investment Verdict: ☐ Buy ☐ Hold ☐ Avoid

Notes: _____

_____

_____

ABUJA (FCT)

Central Business District (Maitama/Asokoro/Wuse)

- Current Rental Yield: _____% annually
- 3-Year Capital Appreciation: _____%
- Entry Cost Range: ₦ _____ to ₦ _____
- Market Maturity: ☐ Emerging ☐ Growing ☐ Mature ☐ Saturated
- Infrastructure Rating: _____/10
- ROI Potential: ☐ High ☐ Medium ☐ Low

Investment Verdict: ☐ Buy ☐ Hold ☐ Avoid

Notes: _____

_____

_____

Satellite Towns (Kubwa/Lugbe/Kuje)

- Current Rental Yield: _____% annually
- 3-Year Capital Appreciation: _____%
- Entry Cost Range: ₦ _____ to ₦ _____
- Market Maturity: ☐ Emerging ☐ Growing ☐ Mature ☐ Saturated
- Infrastructure Rating: _____/10
- ROI Potential: ☐ High ☐ Medium ☐ Low

Investment Verdict: ☐ Buy ☐ Hold ☐ Avoid

Notes: _____

_____

_____

SECONDARY MARKETS ANALYSIS

PORT HARCOURT

- Market Size: _____
- Key Economic Drivers: _____
- Investment Threshold: ₦ _____
- Infrastructure Development: _____/10
- Risk Level: ☐ Low ☐ Medium ☐ High
- Recommendation: ☐ Invest Now ☐ Monitor ☐ Avoid

Notes: _____
_____
_____

KANO

- Market Size: _____
- Key Economic Drivers: _____
- Investment Threshold: ₦ _____
- Infrastructure Development: _____/10
- Risk Level: ☐ Low ☐ Medium ☐ High
- Recommendation: ☐ Invest Now ☐ Monitor ☐ Avoid

Notes: _____
_____
_____

IBADAN

- Market Size: _____
- Key Economic Drivers: _____
- Investment Threshold: ₦ _____
- Infrastructure Development: _____/10
- Risk Level: ☐ Low ☐ Medium ☐ High
- Recommendation: ☐ Invest Now ☐ Monitor ☐ Avoid

Notes: _____
_____
_____

EMERGING MARKET OPPORTUNITIES

LOCATION 1: _____

Growth Catalysts:

_____

_____

_____

- Investment Timeline: _____ years
- Risk Assessment: ☐ Speculative ☐ Calculated ☐ Conservative
- Potential Annual Returns: _____%
- Entry Point: ₦ _____

Watch Indicators:

_____

_____

_____

LOCATION 2: _____

Growth Catalysts:

_____

_____

_____

- Investment Timeline: _____ years
- Risk Assessment: ☐ Speculative ☐ Calculated ☐ Conservative
- Potential Annual Returns: _____ %
- Entry Point: ₦ _____

Watch Indicators:

_____

_____

_____

LOCATION 3: _____

Growth Catalysts:

_____

_____

_____

- Investment Timeline: _____ years
- Risk Assessment: ☐ Speculative ☐ Calculated ☐ Conservative
- Potential Annual Returns: _____ %
- Entry Point: ₦ _____

Watch Indicators:

_____

_____

_____

INVESTMENT PRIORITY MATRIX

Rank	Location	Entry Cost	ROI	Risk	Infrastructure	Priority Score
1	_____	₦_____	__%	__/5	__/10	__/25
2	_____	₦_____	__%	__/5	__/10	__/25
3	_____	₦_____	__%	__/5	__/10	__/25
4	_____	₦_____	__%	__/5	__/10	__/25
5	_____	₦_____	__%	__/5	__/10	__/25

TOP 3 INVESTMENT TARGETS

#1 PRIORITY LOCATION: _____

Why: _____

Target Entry Date: _____

Budget Allocated: ₦ _____

#2 PRIORITY LOCATION: _____

Why: _____

Target Entry Date: _____

Budget Allocated: ₦ _____

#3 PRIORITY LOCATION: _____

Why: _____

Target Entry Date: _____

Budget Allocated: ₦ _____

RESEARCH UPDATE SCHEDULE

Quarterly Review Dates:

- Q1: _____
- Q2: _____
- Q3: _____
- Q4: _____

Annual Deep Dive Date: _____

Market Alert Triggers:

- Major infrastructure announcements
- Policy changes affecting property investment
- Significant market price movements (+/- 20%)
- New development corridors announced

CHAPTER 7

TEAM BUILDING TEMPLATE

FROM THE BOOK:

The single most critical success factor in diaspora property investment isn't your budget, your location choice, or even your legal knowledge—it's the quality of your professional team. Attempting DIY property investment from abroad is financial suicide. You need eyes on the ground, boots on the property, and expertise in local markets, legal processes, and property management. But hiring the wrong team is almost as dangerous as having no team at all.

This chapter provides a systematic framework for assembling your core investment team: real estate agent, legal counsel, property manager, accountant, and local support network. For each position, you'll evaluate multiple candidates, check references, verify credentials, and establish clear performance metrics before engagement. Your team should work together seamlessly, with defined communication protocols and accountability measures. Remember: you're not just hiring service providers—you're building a business partnership that will protect and grow your wealth for years or decades. Invest time upfront in team selection, and you'll save yourself years of stress and costly mistakes. Rush this process, and you'll pay for it—guaranteed.

TEAM BUILDING TEMPLATE

Team Assembly Timeline: _____

Budget for Professional Services: $ _____ / ₦ _____

REAL ESTATE AGENT/PROPERTY CONSULTANT

CANDIDATE EVALUATION

CANDIDATE 1:

- Name: _____
- License Number: _____
- Years of Experience: _____
- Specialization: _____
- Diaspora Client Experience: ☐ Yes ☐ No
- Client References: ☐ Contacted ☐ Verified
- Fee Structure: _____
- Availability: _____
- Rating: _____/10

Reference Check Notes:

_____

_____

_____

CANDIDATE 2:

- Name: _____
- License Number: _____
- Years of Experience: _____
- Specialization: _____
- Diaspora Client Experience: ☐ Yes ☐ No
- Client References: ☐ Contacted ☐ Verified
- Fee Structure: _____
- Availability: _____
- Rating: _____/10

Reference Check Notes:

_____

_____

_____

CANDIDATE 3:

- Name: _____
- License Number: _____
- Years of Experience: _____
- Specialization: _____
- Diaspora Client Experience: ☐ Yes ☐ No
- Client References: ☐ Contacted ☐ Verified
- Fee Structure: _____
- Availability: _____
- Rating: _____/10

Reference Check Notes:

_____

_____

_____

SELECTED AGENT: _____

Contract Terms: _____

Performance Metrics:

- Response Time: Within _____ hours
- Property Viewings: Minimum _____ per month
- Market Updates: _____ frequency
- Weekly Check-ins: ☐ Yes ☐ No
- **Contract Signed:** ☐ Yes ☐ No **Date:** _____

LEGAL COUNSEL

LAWYER EVALUATION

CANDIDATE 1:

- Name: _____
- Bar Registration Number: _____
- Law Firm: _____
- Property Law Experience: _____ years
- Diaspora Client Experience: ☐ Yes ☐ No
- Fee Schedule: _____
- Response Time: _____
- Rating: _____/10

Services Offered:

- Title verification
- Contract review
- Due diligence support
- Governor's consent processing
- Property registration
- Ongoing legal advisory

SELECTED LAWYER: _____

Retainer Agreement: ☐ Signed ☐ Pending

Scope of Services:

Fee Structure:

- Title Search: ₦ _____
- Contract Review: ₦ _____
- Registration Support: ₦ _____
- Retainer (if applicable): ₦ _____ /month

Contract Signed: ☐ Yes ☐ No **Date:** _____

PROPERTY MANAGEMENT COMPANY

MANAGEMENT COMPANY EVALUATION

Criteria	Company 1	Company 2	Company 3
Company Name			
License Number			
Years in Business			
Properties Managed			
Technology Platform	__/10	__/10	__/10
Monthly Fee (% of rent)	___%	___%	___%
Tenant Screening	☐ Yes ☐ No	☐ Yes ☐ No	☐ Yes ☐ No
Maintenance Services	☐ Yes ☐ No	☐ Yes ☐ No	☐ Yes ☐ No
Financial Reporting	☐ Yes ☐ No	☐ Yes ☐ No	☐ Yes ☐ No
Emergency Response	☐ 24/7 ☐ Limited	☐ 24/7 ☐ Limited	☐ 24/7 ☐ Limited
Client References	__/10	__/10	__/10
TOTAL SCORE	__/30	__/30	__/30

SELECTED PROPERTY MANAGER: _____

Contract Duration: _____ years

Services Included:

- Rent collection
- Tenant management
- Maintenance coordination
- Monthly financial reporting
- Quarterly inspections
- Emergency response
- Lease renewals
- Eviction support (if needed)

Key Performance Indicators:

- Occupancy Rate Target: _____%

- Rent Collection Rate: _____%

- Maintenance Response Time: _____ hours

- Monthly Report Delivery: Day _____ of month

Monthly Fee: _____% of rental income

Contract Signed: ☐ Yes ☐ No **Date:** _____

FINANCIAL SERVICES TEAM

ACCOUNTANT/TAX ADVISOR

- Name: _____
- Professional Body: _____
- Qualifications: _____
- Nigeria Tax Expertise: ☐ Yes ☐ No
- International Client Experience: ☐ Yes ☐ No
- Property Tax Specialization: ☐ Yes ☐ No
- Annual Fee: ₦ _____

Services:

- Tax planning and filing
- Property tax compliance
- Financial reporting
- Investment analysis
- Currency management advice

Contract Signed: ☐ Yes ☐ No **Date:** _____

BANKING RELATIONSHIP

- Nigerian Bank: _____
- Account Type: _____
- Account Number: _____
- Relationship Manager: _____
- Contact Information: _____
- International Transfer Capabilities: ☐ Yes ☐ No
- Online Banking: ☐ Activated
- Mobile App: ☐ Installed

Date Opened: _____

INSURANCE BROKER

- Company/Broker Name: _____
- License Number: _____
- Coverage Types Offered: ☐ Property/Building Insurance
    - Contents Insurance
    - Liability Insurance
    - Loss of Rent Insurance
- Annual Premium Range: ₦ _____
- Claims Processing Record: _____/10
- Contact Information: _____

Policy Effective Date: _____

SUPPORT NETWORK

LOCAL CONTACT PERSON

- Name: _____
- Relationship: _____
- Contact Information: _____
- WhatsApp: _____
- Availability: _____
- Compensation Arrangement: _____

Responsibilities:

- Property viewing assistance
- Document collection
- Emergency response
- Contractor supervision
- Market intelligence

DIASPORA NETWORK

- Community/Investment Group: _____
- Key Contacts: _____
- Meeting Frequency: _____
- Online Platform: _____
- Investment Club Participation: ☐ Yes ☐ No

Benefits:

- Deal flow sharing
- Knowledge exchange
- Group buying power
- Referrals and vetting

TEAM COMMUNICATION PROTOCOLS

Regular Meeting Schedule:

- Agent Check-in: _____ (frequency)
- Lawyer Updates: _____ (frequency)
- Property Manager Reports: _____ (frequency)
- Accountant Reviews: _____ (frequency)
- Full Team Meeting: _____ (frequency)

Emergency Contact Tree:

- **Property Emergency:** _____
- **Legal Emergency:** _____
- **Financial Emergency:** _____

Reporting Requirements:

- Weekly Updates: From _____
- Monthly Reports: From _____
- Quarterly Reviews: With _____

Communication Platforms:

- Primary: _____
- Video Calls: _____
- Document Sharing: _____
- Instant Messaging: _____

TEAM PERFORMANCE MONITORING

QUARTERLY TEAM REVIEW

Team Member	Performance (1-10)	Issues/Concerns	Action Items
Agent	_____		
Lawyer	_____		
Property Manager	_____		
Accountant	_____		

Team Effectiveness Score: _____/40

Review Date: _____ Next Review: _____

ANNUAL TEAM ASSESSMENT

Overall Team Performance: _____/10

Cost vs Value Analysis:

_____

_____

Team Changes Needed:

_____

_____

Professional Development Support Provided:

_____

_____

Assessment Date: _____ **Assessed By:** _____

CHAPTER 8

REMOTE MANAGEMENT CHECKLIST

FROM THE BOOK:

Owning property in Nigeria while living in London, New York, Toronto, or Sydney presents unique management challenges. You can't drive by to check on your investment. You can't meet tenants face-to-face. You can't personally oversee repairs or renovations. This geographic distance creates vulnerability—unless you implement systematic remote management protocols.

The Remote Management Checklist establishes the technology infrastructure, financial systems, tenant protocols, and maintenance schedules that enable successful absentee ownership. From property management software and security cameras to automated rent collection and preventive maintenance schedules, every element is designed to give you visibility, control, and peace of mind from thousands of miles away. The key is creating redundancy: multiple people, systems, and checkpoints that ensure nothing falls through the cracks. Remote management isn't about doing everything yourself from abroad—it's about building systems that work whether you're checking in daily or taking a month-long vacation. Property investment should create freedom, not become a second full-time job. These systems make that possible.

REMOTE MANAGEMENT CHECKLIST

Property Information:

- Property Address: _____
- Property Type: _____
- Current Status: ☐ Occupied ☐ Vacant
- Management Start Date: _____
- Primary Manager: _____

TECHNOLOGY INFRASTRUCTURE

PROPERTY MANAGEMENT SOFTWARE

- Platform Name: _____
- Monthly Cost: $ _____ / ₦ _____
- Login Credentials: _____ (store securely)

Features Included:

- Rent collection
- Maintenance request tracking
- Financial reporting
- Tenant communication
- Document storage
- Expense tracking
- Automated reminders

Setup Complete: ☐ Yes ☐ No **Date:** _____

COMMUNICATION SYSTEMS

- Primary Platform: _____
- Video Conferencing: _____
- Instant Messaging: _____
- File Sharing: _____
- Emergency Contact Method: _____

All Systems Tested: ☐ Yes ☐ No **Date:** _____

MONITORING TECHNOLOGY

Security & Surveillance:

- Security Cameras: ☐ Installed ☐ Planned ☐ Not needed
    - Provider: _____
    - Monthly Cost: ₦ _____
    - Remote Access: ☐ Yes ☐ No
- Smart Home Systems: ☐ Installed ☐ Planned ☐ Not needed
    - Type: _____
    - Features: _____
- Utility Monitoring: ☐ Installed ☐ Planned ☐ Not needed
    - Services Monitored: _____
- Access Control: ☐ Installed ☐ Planned ☐ Not needed
    - System Type: _____

FINANCIAL MANAGEMENT SYSTEMS

BANKING AND PAYMENTS

- Nigerian Bank Account: _____
- Account Number: _____
- Online Banking Access: ☐ Yes ☐ No
- Mobile App Installed: ☐ Yes ☐ No
- Automatic Rent Collection: ☐ Set up ☐ Pending
- International Transfer Method: _____
- Currency Exchange Strategy: _____

Payment Instructions Documented: ☐ Yes ☐ No

EXPENSE MANAGEMENT

Monthly Budgets:

- Operating Expenses: ₦ _____
- Emergency Repair Fund: ₦ _____
- Capital Improvement Fund: ₦ _____
- Property Tax Reserve: ₦ _____
- **Total Monthly Allocation:** ₦ _____

Expense Tracking System: _____

FINANCIAL REPORTING SCHEDULE

- Monthly Statements: ☐ Set up ☐ Pending

- Statement Delivery Date: Day _____ of month

- Quarterly Reviews: ☐ Scheduled

- Review Dates: Q1_____ Q2_____ Q3_____ Q4_____

- Annual Tax Preparation: ☐ Arranged

- Tax Filing Deadline: _____

- Audit Requirements: _____

TENANT MANAGEMENT PROTOCOLS

TENANT SCREENING PROCESS

Standard Requirements:

- Income verification (3x monthly rent minimum)
- Employment verification
- Previous landlord references (minimum 2)
- Identity verification
- Guarantor requirement (if applicable)
- Security deposit (specify amount: ₦_____)
- Background check

Screening Responsibility: _____

LEASE MANAGEMENT

- Standard Lease Term: _____ months
- Rent Review Schedule: _____ annually
- Rent Increase Cap: _____%
- Maintenance Responsibilities: _____
- Termination Notice Period: _____ days
- Lease Renewal Process: _____

Lease Template Approved by Lawyer: ☐ Yes ☐ No

TENANT COMMUNICATION

- Primary Contact Method: _____
- Response Time Commitment: _____ hours
- Emergency Procedures: _____
- Complaint Resolution Process: _____
- Regular Check-in Frequency: _____

Communication Protocol Documented: ☐ Yes ☐ No

MAINTENANCE MANAGEMENT

PREVENTIVE MAINTENANCE SCHEDULE

Maintenance Task	Frequency	Last Completed	Next Due	Responsible Party	Cost (₦)
HVAC servicing	Quarterly	_____	_____	_____	_____
Plumbing inspection	Semi-annual	_____	_____	_____	_____
Electrical check	Annual	_____	_____	_____	_____
Roof inspection	Annual	_____	_____	_____	_____
Painting touch-up	Every 2 years	_____	_____	_____	_____
Security system check	Monthly	_____	_____	_____	_____
Generator service	Quarterly	_____	_____	_____	_____
Water tank cleaning	Semi-annual	_____	_____	_____	_____

Maintenance Calendar Setup: ☐ Complete ☐ Pending

APPROVED VENDOR NETWORK

Electrician:

- Name: _____
- Contact: _____
- Hourly Rate: ₦ _____
- Emergency Rate: ₦ _____
- Rating: _____/10

Plumber:

- Name: _____
- Contact: _____
- Hourly Rate: ₦ _____
- Emergency Rate: ₦ _____
- Rating: _____/10

HVAC Technician:

- Name: _____
- Contact: _____
- Service Rate: ₦ _____
- Rating: _____/10

Painter:

- Name: _____
- Contact: _____
- Rate per sqm: ₦ _____
- Rating: _____/10

General Contractor:

- Name: _____
- Contact: _____
- Hourly Rate: ₦ _____
- Rating: _____/10

Security Company:

- Name: _____
- Contact: _____
- Monthly Fee: ₦ _____
- Services: _____

All Vendors Vetted: ☐ Yes ☐ No **Date:** _____

MONTHLY MANAGEMENT CHECKLIST

WEEK 1: FINANCIAL REVIEW

- Verify rent payment received
- Check bank deposits
- Review previous month expenses
- Approve pending payments
- Update financial tracking

Completed: ☐ Yes ☐ No **Date:** _____

WEEK 2: MAINTENANCE REVIEW

- Review maintenance requests
- Check work order status
- Verify preventive maintenance schedule
- Assess vendor performance
- Approve emergency repairs

Completed: ☐ Yes ☐ No **Date:** _____

WEEK 3: TENANT RELATIONS

- Review tenant communications
- Check lease compliance
- Address any concerns
- Plan lease renewals (if applicable)
- Tenant satisfaction check

Completed: ☐ Yes ☐ No **Date:** _____

WEEK 4: STRATEGIC REVIEW

- Review property value/market conditions
- Assess team performance
- Update investment tracking

- Plan next month priorities
- Schedule quarterly call (if due)

Completed: ☐ Yes ☐ No **Date:** _____

ANNUAL PROPERTY REVIEW

PHYSICAL INSPECTION

- Professional inspection scheduled
- Structural assessment completed
- Systems functionality verified
- Cosmetic condition evaluated
- Repairs/improvements identified

Inspection Date: _____ **Inspector:** _____

FINANCIAL PERFORMANCE

- Total income vs budget reviewed
- Total expenses vs budget reviewed
- Actual vs projected ROI calculated
- Cash flow analysis completed
- Tax preparation initiated

Review Date: _____ **Reviewed By:** _____

STRATEGIC ASSESSMENT

- Hold vs sell analysis conducted
- Rent increase consideration reviewed
- Refinancing opportunities assessed
- Portfolio expansion plans updated
- Investment goals progress measured

Assessment Date: _____ Next Assessment: _____

CHAPTER 9

YOUR 90-DAY IMPLEMENTATION JOURNEY

FROM THE BOOK:

Knowledge without implementation is worthless. You can read every property investment book published, attend every seminar, and complete every worksheet—but if you don't take systematic action, you'll never build wealth through real estate. The 90-Day Implementation Journey transforms you from uncertain beginner to deal-ready investor through structured, progressive action.

This isn't a generic timeline—it's a battle-tested roadmap used by hundreds of successful diaspora investors. Each week builds on the previous one, moving you through foundation building (financial preparation, team research), knowledge acquisition (market analysis, legal education), strategic planning (location selection, financing strategy), and execution readiness (property evaluation, due diligence mastery). The timeline is aggressive but achievable for committed investors who dedicate 5-10 hours per week. Some phases may take longer depending on your starting point and available time, but the sequence remains constant. By Day 90, you should be actively evaluating properties with confidence—or have already made your first investment. The difference between dreamers and investors is simple: investors execute. Let's get you from dreaming to doing.

YOUR 90-DAY IMPLEMENTATION JOURNEY

Start Date: _____

Target Completion Date: _____

Weekly Time Commitment: _____ hours

Accountability Partner: _____

PHASE 1:

WEEK 1: ASSESSMENT & COMMITMENT

Focus: Self-evaluation and goal setting

Day 1-2: Self-Assessment

- Complete Self-Assessment Tracker (Chapter 1)
- Calculate your investment readiness score
- Identify your top 3 improvement areas
- Set realistic investment timeline

Your Readiness Score: _____/140

Priority Areas:

1. _____
2. _____
3. _____

Day 3-4: Financial Foundation Review

- Calculate available investment capital
- Review emergency fund status
- Assess debt-to-income ratio
- Open Nigerian bank account (if needed)
- Research currency transfer providers

Available Capital: $ _____ / ₦ _____

Action Items:

_____

_____

_____

Day 5-7: Goal Setting & Planning

- Define your investment objectives
- Set 1-year and 5-year property goals
- Establish budget for professional services
- Create dedicated investment folder/files
- Schedule weekly review time in calendar

Primary Investment Goal:

Timeline: _____

Budget Allocated: $ _____ / ₦ _____

WEEK 1 REFLECTION:

What did I accomplish? _____

Biggest challenge? _____

Next week priority? _____

WEEK 2: TEAM RESEARCH

Focus: Identifying potential team members

Day 8-10: Real Estate Agent Research

- Identify 5+ potential agents online
- Request credentials and client references
- Review agent profiles and specializations
- Prepare interview questions
- Schedule initial consultations (minimum 3)

Agents to Interview:

1. _____
2. _____
3. _____

Day 11-13: Legal Counsel Research

- Identify 3-5 property lawyers
- Verify Nigerian Bar Association membership
- Check property law specialization
- Request fee schedules
- Prepare legal consultation questions

Lawyers to Interview:

1. _____
2. _____
3. _____

Day 14: Property Manager Research

- Research 3+ property management companies
- Review online reviews and testimonials
- Request service offerings and fee structures
- Prepare evaluation criteria
- Document findings in Team Building Template

Property Managers to Evaluate:

1. _____
2. _____
3. _____

WEEK 2 REFLECTION:

What did I accomplish? _____

Biggest challenge? _____

Next week priority? _____

WEEK 3: MARKET EDUCATION

Focus: Understanding Nigerian property market

Day 15-17: Location Research

- Read Chapter 3 and 6 of main book thoroughly
- Complete 5-Point Location Scorecard for Lagos
- Complete 5-Point Location Scorecard for Abuja
- Research property prices in target areas
- Join Nigerian property Facebook groups/forums

Top 3 Locations Identified:

1. _____
2. _____
3. _____

Day 18-19: Legal Education

- Read Chapter 4 of main book thoroughly
- Research Certificate of Occupancy process
- Understand Governor's Consent requirements
- Review sample purchase agreements online
- Watch YouTube videos on title verification

Key Legal Concerns Noted:

_____

_____

_____

Day 20-21: Team Interviews

- Conduct agent interviews (via phone/video)
- Conduct lawyer consultations
- Compare fee structures and services
- Check references thoroughly
- Begin preliminary selections

Interview Notes:

_____

_____

_____

WEEK 3 REFLECTION:

What did I accomplish? _____

Biggest challenge? _____

Next week priority? _____

PHASE 1 CHECKPOINT:

- Self-assessment complete
- Financial foundation reviewed
- Minimum 3 agents interviewed
- Minimum 2 lawyers consulted
- Market research initiated
- Legal education ongoing

Phase 1 Completion: _____% **Date:** _____

PHASE 2: KNOWLEDGE & NETWORK (DAYS 22-42)

WEEK 4: DEEP DIVE - MARKET ANALYSIS

Focus: Comprehensive market understanding

Day 22-24: DPF Hotspot Radar

- Complete Hotspot Radar Tool for all primary markets
- Research rental yields in target areas
- Analyze 3-year capital appreciation trends
- Review infrastructure development plans
- Document findings in Chapter 6

Market Analysis Summary:

_____

_____

_____

Day 25-27: Property Listings Review

- Browse PropertyPro.ng for target areas
- Review ToLet.com.ng listings
- Check PrivateProperty.com.ng
- Create spreadsheet of interesting properties
- Note price ranges and property types

Properties of Interest: _____

Average Price Range: ₦ _____ to ₦ _____

Day 28: Due Diligence Study

- Review Due Diligence Templates (Chapter 2)
- Study document verification checklist
- Research Land Registry search process

- Understand property inspection requirements
- Create personal due diligence workflow

Due Diligence Workflow Created: ☐ Yes ☐ No

WEEK 4 REFLECTION:

What did I accomplish? _____

Biggest challenge? _____

Next week priority? _____

WEEK 5: FINANCING STRATEGY

Focus: Determining optimal funding approach

Day 29-31: Financing Options Analysis

- Complete Financing Strategy Planner (Chapter 5)
- Compare cash vs payment plan scenarios
- Research Nigerian bank mortgage rates
- Calculate total investment costs
- Determine currency transfer strategy

Preferred Financing Approach:

Total Budget Required: ₦ _____

Day 32-34: Currency & Transfer Research

- Compare Wise, Remitly, WorldRemit rates
- Open accounts with preferred provider(s)
- Conduct test transfer (small amount)
- Document transfer fees and timelines
- Plan currency hedging strategy (if applicable)

Selected Transfer Provider: _____

Average Fee: _____% **Transfer Time:** _____ days

Day 35: Financial Projections

- Calculate expected rental yield
- Project 5-year ROI scenarios
- Account for maintenance costs
- Include currency fluctuation buffer
- Create financial model spreadsheet

Projected Annual ROI: _____%

Break-even Timeline: _____ years

WEEK 5 REFLECTION:

What did I accomplish? _____

Biggest challenge? _____

Next week priority? _____

WEEK 6: TEAM FINALIZATION

Focus: Locking in professional team

Day 36-38: Team Selection & Contracts

- Select final real estate agent
- Negotiate and sign agent agreement
- Select final legal counsel
- Sign retainer/engagement letter
- Finalize property manager (if applicable)

Team Locked In: ☐ Agent ☐ Lawyer ☐ Property Manager

Total Team Costs: ₦ _____ annually

Day 39-41: Team Coordination Setup

- Create team communication protocol
- Set up WhatsApp group or Slack channel

- Schedule regular team check-ins
- Establish reporting requirements
- Conduct first team coordination call

First Team Meeting: _____ (date)

Communication Platform: _____

Day 42: Support Network Development

- Identify local contact person
- Join diaspora investment communities
- Connect with 3+ fellow investors
- Share contact information
- Establish peer support system

Local Contact: _____

Diaspora Network: _____

WEEK 6 REFLECTION:

What did I accomplish? _____

Biggest challenge? _____

Next week priority? _____

PHASE 2 CHECKPOINT:

- Market analysis complete for 5+ locations
- Financing strategy determined
- Currency transfer system operational
- Professional team fully assembled
- Communication protocols established
- Support network activated

Phase 2 Completion: _____% **Date:** _____

PHASE 3: STRATEGIC EXECUTION (DAYS 43-70)
WEEK 7: PROPERTY IDENTIFICATION

Focus: Finding potential investments

Day 43-45: Property Search Activation

- Provide agent with detailed criteria
- Set up property alerts online
- Request virtual viewings from agent
- Review 10+ property listings
- Shortlist 5-7 properties for evaluation

Properties Shortlisted: _____

Criteria Used:

_____

_____

_____

Day 46-48: Virtual Property Viewings

- Conduct virtual tours via video call
- Request additional photos/videos
- Ask detailed questions about properties
- Review neighborhood via Google Maps
- Document observations systematically

Viewings Completed: _____

Top 3 Properties After Viewings:

1. _____
2. _____
3. _____

Day 49: Property Comparison

- Complete Risk Assessment for each property
- Use 5-Point Location Scorecard
- Compare using Property Comparison Matrix
- Calculate ROI for each option
- Narrow to top 2-3 properties

Final Shortlist:

1. _____ (Score: _____/490)

2. _____ (Score: _____/490)

WEEK 7 REFLECTION:

What did I accomplish? _____

Biggest challenge? _____

Next week priority? _____

WEEK 8: DUE DILIGENCE INITIATION

Focus: Comprehensive property verification

Day 50-52: Document Request & Review

- Request all property documents from seller
- Verify Certificate of Occupancy with lawyer
- Review survey plan
- Check building plan approval
- Request tax clearance certificates

Documents Received: _____/8

Initial Legal Review: ☐ Complete ☐ Pending

Day 53-55: Title Verification

- Lawyer conducts Land Registry search
- Verify chain of title
- Check for encumbrances/liens
- Confirm no pending litigation
- Review Governor's Consent status

Title Status: ☐ Clear ☐ Issues Identified ☐ Pending

Issues (if any):

_____

_____

Day 56: Developer/Seller Background Check

- Verify company registration (CAC)
- Research developer track record
- Check completed projects
- Contact previous buyers
- Review online reputation

Developer Rating: _____/10

Proceed? ☐ Yes ☐ No ☐ Conditional

WEEK 8 REFLECTION:

What did I accomplish? _____

Biggest challenge? _____

Next week priority? _____

WEEK 9: PROPERTY INSPECTION & VALUATION

Focus: Physical assessment and pricing verification

Day 57-59: Physical Inspection

- Arrange professional inspection (via agent)
- Complete Property Inspection Checklist
- Document condition with photos/videos
- Assess necessary repairs/improvements
- Evaluate overall property quality

Overall Property Rating: _____/10

Repair Costs Estimated: ₦ _____

Day 60-62: Market Valuation

- Compare prices of similar properties
- Review recent sales in area
- Assess property's competitive position
- Determine fair market value
- Identify negotiation leverage

Asking Price: ₦ _____

Fair Market Value: ₦ _____

Negotiation Room: _____%

Day 63: Investment Decision

- Review all due diligence findings
- Consult with team (agent, lawyer)
- Complete final Risk Assessment
- Make GO/NO-GO decision
- Document rationale

DECISION: ☐ Proceed ☐ Negotiate ☐ Walk Away

Rationale:

_____

_____

_____

WEEK 9 REFLECTION:

What did I accomplish? _____

Biggest challenge? _____

Next week priority? _____

WEEK 10: NEGOTIATION & OFFER

Focus: Securing favorable terms

Day 64-66: Offer Preparation

- Determine maximum offer price
- Decide on payment structure
- Define contingencies clearly
- Draft offer letter with lawyer
- Prepare negotiation strategy

Initial Offer: ₦ _____

Payment Structure: _____

Day 67-69: Negotiation Process

- Submit formal offer through agent
- Respond to counteroffers strategically
- Negotiate price, terms, timeline
- Secure concessions where possible
- Reach preliminary agreement

Final Agreed Price: ₦ _____

Key Terms:

_____

_____

_____

Day 70: Purchase Agreement Review

- Lawyer reviews purchase agreement
- Verify all negotiated terms included
- Clarify any ambiguous clauses
- Confirm payment schedule
- Approve agreement for signing

Agreement Approved: ☐ Yes ☐ No

Signing Date: _____

WEEK 10 REFLECTION:

What did I accomplish? _____

Biggest challenge? _____

Next week priority? _____

PHASE 3 CHECKPOINT:

- Property identified and evaluated
- Comprehensive due diligence completed
- Physical inspection conducted
- Market valuation performed
- Offer submitted and negotiated
- Purchase agreement reviewed and approved

Phase 3 Completion: _____% **Date:** _____

PHASE 4: TRANSACTION COMPLETION (DAYS 71-90)
WEEK 11-12: CLOSING PROCESS

Focus: Finalizing the investment

Day 71-73: Initial Payment

- Transfer deposit to escrow/seller
- Confirm receipt with agent
- Obtain payment receipt
- Update payment tracking
- Notify lawyer of payment completion

Deposit Amount: ₦ _____

Date Paid: _____

Day 74-77: Documentation Finalization

- Sign purchase agreement
- Execute power of attorney (if applicable)
- Complete all required forms
- Submit Governor's Consent application
- Initiate property registration process

Documents Signed: _____

Governor's Consent: ☐ Submitted ☐ Pending

Day 78-80: Payment Completion

- Execute remaining payments per schedule
- Maintain payment records
- Confirm each payment receipt
- Update financial tracking
- Verify balance cleared

Total Paid to Date: ₦ _____

Balance Remaining: ₦ _____

Day 81-83: Property Handover

- Conduct final inspection
- Verify property condition
- Receive keys and access codes
- Transfer utilities to your name
- Update property insurance

Handover Date: _____

Property Condition: ☐ Satisfactory ☐ Issues Noted

Day 84-86: Post-Purchase Setup

- Engage property manager (if rental)
- Set up remote management systems
- Install security/monitoring (if planned)
- Complete Remote Management Checklist
- Establish tenant search (if applicable)

Management Systems Active: ☐ Yes ☐ No

Day 87-90: CELEBRATION & REFLECTION

- Update investment portfolio records
- Calculate actual ROI projections
- Schedule ongoing management reviews
- Thank your team
- **CELEBRATE YOUR ACHIEVEMENT!**

90-DAY JOURNEY COMssPLETE!

Completion Date: _____

Property Acquired: _____

Purchase Price: ₦ _____

Total Investment (including costs): ₦ _____

Projected Annual ROI: _____%

JOURNEY REFLECTION:

Biggest Lesson Learned:

_____

_____

Most Valuable Resource:

_____

Advice for Future Investors:

_____

_____

Next Investment Target Date: _____

_____

ALTERNATIVE: NOT READY TO BUY YET?

If you haven't purchased by Day 90, that's okay!

- I'm still in due diligence on a specific property
- I'm waiting for better market conditions
- I need more time to accumulate capital
- I'm still building my knowledge/network

Revised Timeline:

- Complete team assembly by: _____
- Begin property search by: _____
- Target purchase date: _____

What I accomplished in 90 days:

_____

_____

_____

Next 90-day goals:

_____

_____

_____

_____

_____

_____

_____

_____

_____

CHAPTER 10

PROGRESS TRACKING & WINS TRACKER

MONTHLY PROGRESS DASHBOARD

Month: _____ Year: _____

INVESTMENT READINESS SCORE

Current Score: _____/140 (Target: 102)

Change from Last Month: +/- _____

Areas Improved:
_____

Areas Needing Focus:
_____

_____

MILESTONE TRACKER

Milestone	Target Date	Status	Actual Date
Complete Self-Assessment	_____	☐	_____
Hire Real Estate Agent	_____	☐	_____
Engage Legal Counsel	_____	☐	_____
Complete Location Analysis	_____	☐	_____
Secure Financing	_____	☐	_____
Identify Target Property	_____	☐	_____
Complete Due Diligence	_____	☐	_____
Submit Offer	_____	☐	_____
Sign Purchase Agreement	_____	☐	_____
Complete Payment	_____	☐	_____
Obtain Property Title	_____	☐	_____

Milestones Completed This Month: _____

Total Milestones Completed: _____/11

WINS TRACKER

Celebrate every small victory!

Week 1 Win:

_____

Week 2 Win:

_____

Week 3 Win:

_____

Week 4 Win:

_____

Biggest Win This Month:

_____
_____
_____

CHALLENGES OVERCOME

Challenge Faced **Solution Implemented** **Lesson Learned**

_____

MONTHLY REFLECTION

What went well this month?

_____
_____

What could I improve?

_____
_____

Key insight or learning:

_____
_____

Next month's primary focus:

_____

_____

_____

INVESTMENT METRICS (Once Property Acquired)

Property Address: _____

Purchase Date: _____

Purchase Price: ₦ _____

Current Estimated Value: ₦ _____

Monthly Performance:

Month	Rental Income	Expenses	Net Income	Notes
1	₦_____	₦_____	₦_____	
2	₦_____	₦_____	₦_____	
3	₦_____	₦_____	₦_____	
6	₦_____	₦_____	₦_____	
12	₦_____	₦_____	₦_____	

Current ROI: _____%

Occupancy Rate: _____%

Tenant Status: _____

ABOUT THE AUTHOR

Abiodun D. Doherty

Legal Practitioner | Real Estate Strategist | Diaspora Investment Advocate

Abiodun D. Doherty is a seasoned legal practitioner, real estate strategist, and trusted voice on diaspora property investment, with over two decades of experience across Nigeria and Australia. He is the Principal Partner of Abiodun D. Doherty & Co., a respected Lagos-based law firm specializing in property law, and the Director of De Kings Global Trading & Services Pty Ltd, which connects Nigerians in the diaspora with education and strategic investment opportunities.

With a unique blend of legal expertise and real-world investment insight, Abiodun has helped hundreds of diaspora clients avoid costly mistakes and invest safely in Nigeria's real estate market. His reputation for integrity, due diligence, and results has made him a go-to advisor in a sector often fraught with fraud and misinformation.

Abiodun has led seminars, coaching programs, and community workshops across major diaspora hubs, empowering Nigerians abroad to build wealth and legacy through smart property investments. His expert insights have been featured in leading Nigerian media, including The Punch, and he is a frequent speaker at conferences and forums focused on diaspora engagement and wealth creation.

He holds a Master of Laws (LL.M.) from the University of Lagos, with specialization in Company, Commercial, and Property Law, and is also a licensed Australian Realtor—giving him rare cross-border expertise in international property transactions.

Whether you're a first-time buyer or a seasoned investor, Abiodun's mission is simple: to help you invest back home, confidently and securely.

Contact Information:

Website: www.diasporapropertyformula.com
Email: info@diasporapropertyformula.com

JOIN THE ACADEMY

Go Further — Join The Diaspora Property Formula™ Academy

Turn this workbook into results.

You have the knowledge. Now it's time for execution.

The **Diaspora Property Formula™ Academy** gives you step-by-step video lessons, proven templates, and expert guidance to execute your first (or next) safe property deal in Nigeria.

CHOOSE YOUR PATH:

DPF FOUNDATIONS

Perfect for your first property

6 Core Modules | Legal Protection Framework | Property Selection System | Fraud Prevention Checklist | Team Building Templates | Lifetime Access

Don't miss it! Special discount for founding members.

DPF IMPLEMENTATION ACCELERATOR

MOST POPULAR

For serious investors building a portfolio

8 Advanced Modules | Everything in Foundations PLUS Portfolio Building | Advanced Negotiation | Property Management Systems | Tax Optimization | Scaling Strategies | Lifetime Access

Don't miss it! Special discount for founding members.

BEST VALUE: Bundle both courses and save significantly

THE INNER CIRCLE MASTERMIND

VIP ACCESS

Elite community + personal coaching

Both Courses | 12 Monthly Live Q&A Sessions | Private Community | TWO 60-Min Strategy Calls | Deal Review Service | Legal Templates | Quarterly Market Reports | Signed Hardcover Book | 12-Month VIP Access

Don't miss it! Special discount for founding members.

ENROLL TODAY:

www.diasporapropertyformula.com/academy

Use code **WORKBOOK2025** for bonus resources

30-Day Money-Back Guarantee

READY TO SECURE YOUR PROPERTY INVESTMENT?

Your Journey from Planning to Profit Starts Now

You've completed the workbook.
You understand the system.
Now execute with expert guidance.

Congratulations on completing this workbook.

Join thousands of diaspora Nigerians who have transformed their property dreams into tangible assets through The Academy.

Where knowledge becomes ownership.
Where planning becomes profit.
Where you finally invest back home—safely.

YOUR SECURE NIGERIAN PROPERTY INVESTMENT IS JUST ONE DECISION AWAY.

Join The Academy. Master the system. Build your wealth.

www.diasporapropertyformula.com/academy

Email: support@diasporapropertyformula.com

Connect with us: Instagram & Facebook: @diasporapropertyformula

Don't miss out on founding member pricing—limited spots available.

© 2025 Abiodun Doherty. All rights reserved.

NOTES & REFLECTIONS

Use this space to capture insights, questions, action items, and reflections as you work through your investment journey.

Date: _____

_____

_____

_____

_____

_____

_____

_____

Date: _____

_____

_____

_____

_____

Date: _____

END OF WORKBOOK

Workbook Complete!
© 2025 Abiodun D. Doherty. All rights reserved.

www.diasporapropertyformula.com

www.ingramcontent.com/pod-product-compliance
Lightning Source LLC
Chambersburg PA
CBHW061121070526
44583CB00028B/3352